Copyright © 2023 by Cyril & Dorise Publishing

All rights reserved.

No part of this publication may be reproduced, distributed, or transmitted in any form or by any means, including photocopying, recording, or other electronic or mechanical methods, without the prior written permission of the publisher, except in the case of brief quotations embodied in critical reviews and certain other non-commercial uses permitted by copyright law.

For permission requests, write to the publisher, addressed "Attention:
Permissions Coordinator," at the address below.

Harmony Close,
Kewtown,
Providenciales
Turks & Caicos Islands

ISBN: 9781739369156

https://www.cyrilanddorsiepublishing.com/

IT'S
IN
THE
BREAKING

TABLE OF CONTENTS

I	You Will Never Understand The Making Until You've Dealt With The Breaking	1
II	Salvation-God's Plan For Mankind	5
III	Don't Get Distracted	9
IV	We Shall Recover All	13
V	Don't Let the Enemy Stop You	16
VI	Fear	18
VII	The Fire of God	24
VIII	Are You Ready?	28
IX	The Fight Is Over	31
X	Journal	36

It's In The Breaking

Holy Spirit, I pray for the individuals or whomsoever is reading this book to be blessed and that their understanding is enlightened, hope restored and every feeling of illusion be put to shame through the blood of Jesus.

Amen.

CHAPTER 1

You Will Never Understand the Making Until You've Dealt With the Breaking

Chapter One
You'll Never Understand the Making Until You've Dealt with the Breaking

O God the Lord, the strength of my salvation, thou hast covered my head in the day of battle.
Psalms 140:7

Many today are still straddling after years of mission on the battlefield, singing in the choir, preaching in the pulpit, and perhaps teaching Bible Study. Whatever positions they may hold are still handicapped and crippled by the enemy straddling them. If we desire to become skilled fighters and stay in the race, we must be able to stand firm on the promises of God's Word and be ready to fight the good fight of faith. Our walk with God must become a testament to all that our lives can minister to from time to time. On top of that, we must be willing to hold high standards of holiness if we are going to stay in the race. We must have the substance and strength to come against all negativity that the enemy will bring our way, and we must know in whom we put our trust.

> *Some trust in chariots, and some in horses: but we will remember the name of the Lord our God.*
>
> **Psalms 20:7**

Every skilled soldier knows their different techniques when it comes to fighting; of course, we should all be ready at all times, looking for the enemy whenever he comes. We must never let him take us unaware. Still, if we are straddling, failing to gain balance, we are bound to be caught off guard and placed in a malfunctioning position that keeps us in a handicapped position that makes us feel isolated and threatened at most times, eventually leading to us throwing in the towel and quitting. I can confess to this. I suffered multiple delays because of it. If we are to defeat this enemy, we must be willing to stand up and fight back!

> *And from the days of John the Baptist until now the kingdom of heaven suffereth violence, and the violent take it by force.*
>
> **Matthew 11:12**

You cannot allow this Spirit of stagnation to stop you from coming forth after many years of service. Have you ever stopped and thought about the things that are holding you back?

It's not a surprise to me! I've been there, too, but I decided to fight back by fair means or force. We must never think that we ought to stay in such positions. Our Lord and Saviour had paid a debt and a price we couldn't pay. He gave His life so that we may be free from any chain the enemy might use against us to bind us.

CHAPTER 2

Salvation - God's Plan For Mankind

Chapter Two- Salvation- God's Plan for Mankind

If we are going to be free from this stronghold, our salvation must never be taken lightly. We cannot afford to let the enemy trick us into believing that what our Saviour has done is a mere thing. To be honest with you, many of us are in the predicament that we are in because we haven't yet come to the realization that the blood of Jesus is not to be taken lightly!

And almost all things are by the law purged with blood; and without shedding of blood is no remission.
Hebrews 9:22

We must never adapt to thinking that we can live victorious lives outside the blood of Jesus being applied to our lives. We often go on as far as placing blame on God for such things as sickness, death, disasters, etc. Furthermore, we must recognize that we owe God and that He doesn't owe us anything; our rebellion and sins separate us from Him.

But your iniquities have separated between you and your God, and your sins have hid his face from you, that he will not hear.
Isaiah 59:2

We must realize that if we are going to be sons and not bastards, we must be willing to exercise our salvation with wisdom and truth. God wants us to be devoted Christians and truthful soldiers on the battlefield, where there's no loophole the enemy cannot enter. In my early walk with God, I can recall the very first time I surrendered to the will of God. It's a time most of us cannot forget; we were purer, and our minds were more open to receiving whatever God had to say. Today many of us are no longer listening to God's voice. Have you ever thought for a moment what perhaps had gone wrong?

4 Nevertheless I have somewhat against thee, because thou hast left thy first love.

5 Remember therefore from whence thou art fallen, and repent, and do the first works; or else I will come unto thee quickly, and will remove thy candlestick out of his place, except thou repent.

Revelation 2:4-5

We must get up and realize that we have and must repent; failure to do so will result in everlasting punishment in hell. I am convinced that many of you are seeing the more incredible picture now and will decide, with the help of God, to return to your first love from whence you fell. Our salvation is our strength, and we lose fellowship with God when it is lost.

CHAPTER 3

Don't Get Distracted

Chapter Three
Don't Get Distracted

Distraction is another tool the enemy uses to keep us from coming into God's perfect will for our lives. Can you recall the good old days when love was our primary focus? It was those days when family and friends were knitted together. There was no need to worry about our neighbors and their children. We disciplined each other's families/children as if they were our own and shared with each other.

Thanksgiving was for children and adults alike - they were satisfied with what they had, whether a rag doll or a good-smelling cup of bush tea! We were happy. We celebrated and fellowshiped together with what we had. Today, we have become so distracted, and the enemy has used this master tool to push us further away from God. Like Lot's wife, many of us have looked back and become pillars of salt. The enemy truly wants us to abort our mission.

Matthew 4:8-10

8 Again, the devil taketh him up into an exceeding high mountain, and sheweth him all the kingdoms of the world, and the glory of them;

9 And saith unto him, All these things will I give thee, if thou wilt fall down and worship me.

10 Then saith Jesus unto him, Get thee hence, Satan: for it is written, Thou shalt worship the Lord thy God, and him only shalt thou serve.

The enemy is wide awake and deceiving many who would make themselves available. He knows how to trick us into believing that he can fix it for us if we serve him. After all, he is the accuser of the brethren, and I am more than convinced that he can make bitter water look sweet, but the result of it will lead to everlasting punishment in hell. Many are suffering today as a result of the many bad choices made based on these deceptive lies he told them.

Friends, you don't have to be a part of the enemy's camp; reject the worldly pleasures that only last for a season and allow the Holy Spirit to fill you with his peace. Don't give in to this enemy called distraction. God has a better plan for you! All our best days lie ahead of us. Our salvation will bring spring forth. We will rejoice, for the battle is not ours but the Lord's. We won't have to fight alone, for the spirit of truth will arise. We can withstand the enemy's oppression because we have the Word of God, our sword.

Oh! Praise His name for the Lord He is God, a God of many names! Yes, He's Jehovah Gibbor, the Lord Mighty in battle. He will fight effectively for us. For the Egyptians we see today, we will see them no more. Tomorrow, He will save us from the hands of our oppressors.

CHAPTER 4
We Shall Recover All

Chapter Four
We Shall Recover All

God wants us to shift from straddling to overcoming. You can do it; I did, and so can you!

4 Nevertheless I have somewhat against thee, because thou hast left thy first love.

5 Remember therefore from whence thou art fallen, and repent, and do the first works; or else I will come unto thee quickly, and will remove thy candlestick out of his place, except thou repent. Revelation 2:4-5

I can recall a dream that I had. I was pretty much young and still in high school. I was about fourteen at the time. In the dream, I saw a golden vessel coming from the west and landing in the east, where I was sitting. To be honest with you, I said west because from where I was sitting in the front, it seemed to have come from over the housetop. However, I watched it descend, and it landed exactly in front of me, but it fell to the ground in shambles. I was fascinated with the gold, more than anything, because it was so shiny in its appearance.

There was no gold on this side of planet Earth to compare it to! So I got up, stooped down, and picked up the broken pieces. They weren't that small, so I started to see if I could fix them together. This was unusual; as I fixed a piece, it automatically came together until every piece was returned to its rightful place. I really couldn't comprehend this! I have shared this dream multiple times. At that time, it was not until my process that I realized I was that broken vessel that had to be put back together again. We must be able to overcome any obstacle that the enemy is sending our way. Many like me may have had a similar dream and thought of it as nothing, but in reality, it was your life that God was showing you and that He can give you the strength to fix the many situations you may be facing right now. It is never too late to start putting those pieces together. Your life was meant to glorify God. I am more than convinced that if you get up from doing nothing and exercise your faith, God won't leave you. After all, He is still waiting on you to make the first step.

Jeremiah 18:6

O house of Israel, cannot I do with you as this potter? saith the Lord. Behold, as the clay is in the potter's hand, so are ye in mine hand, O house of Israel.

CHAPTER 5

Don't Let The Enemy Stop You

Chapter Five
Don't Let The Enemy Stop You

Have you ever noticed that hell and all its agents come up against you when you decide to fight back?

Have you considered what you saw in dreams and visions that you were afraid to speak aloud because you felt no one would believe you? If that's you, it's time to deal with the enemy of fear.

> ***There is no fear in love; but perfect love casteth out fear:***
> ***because fear hath torment.***
> ***He that feareth is not made perfect in love.***
>
> ***1st John 4:18***

CHAPTER 6

Fear

Chapter Six
Fear

Fear is another stronghold that the enemy is using against the many children of God to hold them captive. Like myself, many of you have been imprisoned by this enemy called fear. God had shown you dreams and visions for many years. We refuse to speak of those things that would bring glory to God. Like me, I am convinced you have seen many beautiful things; the enemy does not want you to testify of them. He allows fear to take control of your hearts, and he knows that many out there are waiting and can testify of it.

We must not allow this stronghold to keep us in bondage. I had many encounters with the Holy Spirit, including another dream I mentioned many times while preaching. At some point, I was afraid to speak of it. It was glorious. I could not have allowed the enemy to silence me with it, for God had revealed himself in the clouds with a rainbow above His head. This was quick, in the blink of an eye. I looked again, but it was gone.

He only allowed me to have a quick glimpse. The rainbow above His head stood out; no cloud was so white. I likened it to wool; it was even whiter than it.

These two things caught my eye. There's no cloud of white on this side of the earth like it. Nothing can describe it, yet the enemy wants to fill our hearts with fear not to speak of it. He doesn't want us to mention God's name. Imagine having Him reveal to us His glory, friends. I couldn't keep it; I had to share it, and I am happy I did. Many of you out there may have seen this truth. He had no doubt revealed Himself to you. His hand, feet, and hand parts had stretched out to you, but you were afraid because of the enemy called fear. Let us make up our minds that we will paralyze this enemy forever.

16 But blessed are your eyes, for they see: and your ears, for they hear.

17 For verily I say unto you, That many prophets and righteous men have desired to see those things which ye see, and have not seen them; and to hear those things which ye hear, and have not heard them.

Matthew 13:16-17

We must never become afraid of what we have seen; our lives are testaments of God's truth. We are his hands and feet in the earth. We must cripple this deadly enemy of negative thinking. If we desire to go to our next dimension in God, we must be willing to stand bold in the enemy's face and bring his words to naught. Words are powerful, and they can affect you positively or negatively. I realized this is also a tool that the enemy has been using for a long time to paralyze the growth of many believers. It is so sad that many of us have fallen prey. His goal is to stop the plan of God for our lives by keeping us imbalanced, or should I say straddling, so that he can gain complete control.

Many stories in the Bible speak of the danger of words. One of the more popular ones can be found in 1 Kings 19:2.

> **Then Jezebel sent a messenger unto Elijah, saying, So let the gods do to me, and more also, if I make not thy life as the life of one of them by to morrow about this time.**
>
> **1Kings 19:2**

At the word of Jezebel, Elijah ran and hid himself in a cave. We must never allow the enemy ever to cage us again. Many wounded soldiers are no longer fighting because of one word the enemy spoke. It turned them away, and they refused to endure the cross; they became prisoners in their minds, and many ministries ended because of spoken words. We must get back up and fight. The enemy must not win; he's a loser from the beginning and will be one to the end.

Many are depressed, heartbroken, and malfunctioning and are no longer walking in the true path of righteousness. They are packed with emotions; they sing on the praise team, play the piano, and preach the Word, but there's no yoke-breaking anointing to free many from the stronghold that held them captive for so long. God is looking for genuine, serious soldiers who, like Jeremiah, are not afraid to pluck, root up, and call darkness into light. We must be willing and obedient if we will eat the good of the land. Our salvation is God's ultimate plan for our lives, and we must get back to basics. If we don't, all hope is lost.

We must understand that we cannot graduate without going through the whole process, and so it is with God that our salvation must be our top priority. We must be willing to take the next step.

For many walk, of whom I have told you often, and now tell you even weeping, that they are the enemies of the cross of Christ:

Philippians 3:18

CHAPTER 7

The Fire of God

Chapter Seven
The Fire of God

Have you received the Holy Ghost since you believed? One can never refrain from this topic if we take our next step toward God.

Our salvation was never meant to keep us stagnated but to mature us into becoming what God wants us to be. We ought to glorify God in our temples and receive the glory He has predestined for us since the beginning of time. God desires us to be baptized with the fire of the Holy Ghost. I discussed this topic some years ago, and it was clear to me what the Apostle Paul had to say.

> **For Christ sent me not to baptize, but to preach the gospel: not with wisdom of words, lest the cross of Christ should be made of none effect.**
>
> **1Corinthains 1:17**

God wants to make us great witnesses of His truth. We must receive His truth so that the Holy Spirit can fill our hearts; only then can we truly become great witnesses of God.

God wants to fill us with the spirit of truth that is the Holy Ghost.

We must be fully baptized in truth if we are going to make great disciples. The spirit of truth breaks yokes and strongholds from our lives, and God reveals Himself and His plans to us for our lives. Many believers are still believing that if I find a good church and a good pastor and get submerged in the water, I'm on my way to heaven, but friends, this is a lie from the pits of hell. I used to think the same way. Submerging into the water was not enough to keep me saved.

We must stop allowing the enemy to deceive us. He did it for many years. Many emerge, not realizing that it is fiction told by those who don't understand God's word. If we are going to be real soldiers, we must be willing to study and know the truth of God's word. I know your eyes are opening. Let us move on, get up and fight back.

John 16:13

Howbeit when he, the Spirit of truth, is come, he will guide
you into all truth: for he shall not speak of himself;
but whatsoever he shall hear, that shall he speak: and he will shew you things to come.

CHAPTER 8

Are you ready?

Chapter Eight
Are You Ready?

For the word of God is quick, and powerful, and sharper than any twoedged sword, piercing even to the dividing asunder of soul and spirit, and of the joints and marrow, and is a discerner of the thoughts and intents of the heart.
Hebrews 4:12

You must become a tabernacle in which the word of God can dwell. The building or place of worship made with man's hands doesn't have the power to keep you. It's temporal and subject to change. You must read the scriptures and the word of God daily; in them are the issues of life that are able to keep you. When we understand this, we can rise up and beat the enemy at the many games he has played on us for years. On top of this, we can become great candidates, not stumbling at the word but rather prepared to give every man the answer he seeks.

We must be willing as believers to search the scriptures daily, for in them are the issues of life. We must always be ready to give men an answer and be equipped to face any battle; if you're a soldier and are not equipped, you will definitely lose the fight. The Word of God is our sword.

And a stone of stumbling, and a rock of offence, even to them which stumble at the word, being disobedient: whereunto also they were appointed.
1 Peter 2:8

  There can be multiple reasons for stumbling at the Word; the primary root is disobedience. We must be equipped enough that every demon of hell trying to cross the line must never be able to frustrate us. This also becomes true when we try to quench the Holy Spirit of God by trying to be aware, perhaps, of our words so as not to hurt anyone. Most times, God gives us a word, and we don't want to say it. Friend, whatever the case, the Word of God is sharper than any two-edged sword. I had to learn it the hard way. I am trying to help many of you who are still stumbling at the Word that if we are going to battle in this army, we don't have to fight in our flesh. The God we serve will fight for us; His word inside us makes us bold as a lion; only then can we silence the enemy.

Our enemies are God's enemies when we are in the right standard with him.

Enemies are oppressors; their job is to silence you from coming forth, but if you are to silence them, you must be willing to go all the way with God.

CHAPTER 9

The Fight Is Over

Chapter Nine
The Fight is Over

Ye shall not need to fight in this battle: set yourselves, stand ye still, and see the salvation of the Lord with you O Judah and Jerusalem: fear not, nor be dismayed; to morrow go out against them: for the Lord will be with you.

2 Chronicles 20:17

Friends, when you stay with God, He will stay with you. Your salvation is essential. No more lies; our eyes have been opened. We have come to the realization that it is the enemy that wants us to be handicapped. He had manipulated us into believing many of his fairy tales. But as of now, we are aware of them. No more distractions. The fear is over. No more straddling. You can never understand the making until you have dealt with the breaking!

If we ought to break free from the enemy of straddling and gain balance over the enemy's destructive schemes, we must be willing to stand alone and fight the good fight of faith. We must put on the full armor of God, enabling us to quench all the fiery darts of the evil one and, above all, a shield of never wavering faith.

We must put on the full armor of God, enabling us to quench all the fiery darts of the evil one and, above all, a shield of never-wavering faith. Our minds must be free from all doubt and fear, looking unto Jesus, who is the author and finisher of our faith, knowing that the God who brought us out yesterday is the same God that is able to bring us through right now.

If you are an overcomer, you must have a never-wavering faith, for he that wavers is like a sea wave driven by the wind.

But let him ask in faith, nothing wavering. For he that wavereth is like a wave of the sea driven with the wind and tossed.

James 1:6

Our faith in God must make us overcomers. The straddling or imbalance must be stopped by replacing a wall of never-wavering faith that balances us at each step.

If we must stand the test of time, we must be able to identify the difference and make the necessary changes to survive this enemy straddling.

Above all, taking the shield of faith, wherewith ye shall be able to quench all the fiery darts of the wicked.
Ephesians 6:16

Our salvation is essential, we must not accept the deceit and lies of the enemy. He had placed us in a handicap position in the first place. He wants to keep us in a malfunctioning position forever but we must be able to break free and win the battles of our mind. You can only understand the making once you have dealt with the breaking.

ABOUT
THE AUTHOR

Apostle Rosemary Duncanson is a unique and rare vessel to the body of Christ. Apostle Duncanson was born in the Turks and Caicos Islands; she is a mother, Pastor, and Teacher. Having proclaimed the Word of God for more than three decades, her yoke-breaking anointing has helped many across all spheres of life. Apostle Dunacanson enjoys her outreach ministries and reaches out to as many as possible, calling darkness into light. After many years of pain, hurt, and disappointments, she is proving her ministries entirely and is determined that the enemy will not win. Her determination has given her recognition in every area of her life.

Letters To God

Letters To God

Letters To God

Letters To God

Letters To God

Letters To God

Letters To God

Letters To God

Letters To God

www.ingramcontent.com/pod-product-compliance
Lightning Source LLC
Chambersburg PA
CBHW061147170426
43209CB00011B/1587